GET CRAFTY

MODELS AND BOXES

Vivienne Bolton

DP
DEMPSEY
PARR

Editor
Barbara Segall

Art Direction
Full Steam Ahead

DesignTeam
Design Study

Photography
Patrick Spillane

Photographic Co-ordinator
Liz Spillane

Styling
Bianca Boulton

Project Management
Kate Miles

The publishers would like to thank Inscribe Ltd., Bordon, Hants. for
providing the art materials used in these projects and
Sophie Boulton for her assistance.

First published in 1998 by
Dempsey Parr
Queen Street House, 4-5 Queen Street, Bath
BA1 1HE

24681097531

Copyright © Dempsey Parr 1998

Produced by Miles Kelly Publishing Ltd
Unit 11, Bardfield Centre, Great Bardfield, Essex CM7 4SL

British Library Cataloguing-in-Publication Data
A catalogue record for this book is available from the British Library.

ISBN 1-84084-404-3

Printed in Italy

MODELS AND BOXES

Contents

Creepy Crawly Pots

Caterpillars, ladybugs, butterflies, and flowers make brilliant decorations on small clay pots. These pots are made from air-hardening clay in the shape of insects and flowers and painted in summer colors. They are great fun to make. Have a look around the garden for creatures to inspire you before you begin.

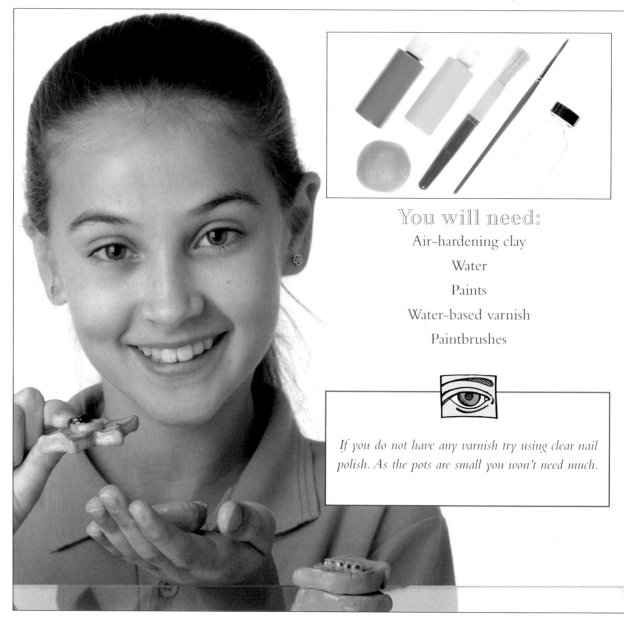

You will need:

Air-hardening clay

Water

Paints

Water-based varnish

Paintbrushes

If you do not have any varnish try using clear nail polish. As the pots are small you won't need much.

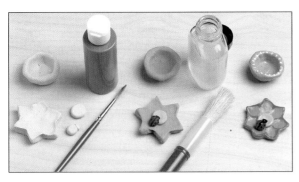

1 First make the bowl of the pot, using your thumbs to shape it. Smooth the clay with your finger tips. When you are happy with the shape, make a lid to fit the bowl. Gently stretch the lid into petal shapes and make a little ladybug from two small clay balls. Use a little water to moisten the base of the ladybug before you attach it to the lid. Leave the pot in a warm airy spot to dry. When it is completely dry, paint it, allowing the paint to dry between colors. When the paint is dry, varnish your pot to give it a professional finish.

2 This ladybug pot is very easy to make. Make the base first, using your thumbs to shape it and smooth the clay with your fingertips. Make a lid to fit the base and leave the pot in a warm airy spot to dry. When it is completely dry, paint the inside and outside black. When the black is dry, paint the ladybug red, then paint on the black dots. You may need to touch up the black when it is dry.

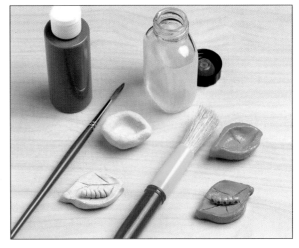

3 The caterpillar on this pot is made from small balls of clay, all joined up with water. When it is dry, decorate the caterpillar in bright colors.

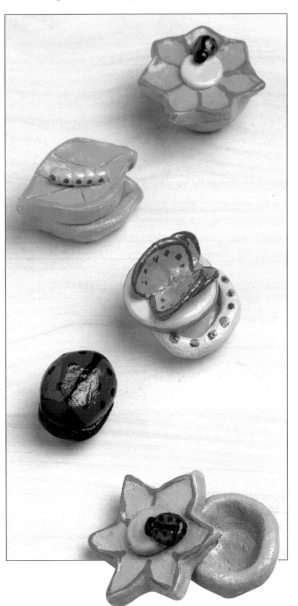

Découpage Boxes

Découpage is the art of decorating boxes with paper cutouts. These boxes have been decorated with pictures cut from wrapping paper. Old magazines are a good source for pictures.

Use a box with a tight lid to decorate for a gardening friend to store seeds in, or decorate to hold special handmade decorations for the Christmas tree.

You will need:

Boxes to decorate

Glue

Newspaper

Paint

Paintbrushes

Scissors

Pictures cut from wrapping paper

Water-based varnish

1 Make sure your chosen box is clean inside. Glue on a layer of newspaper squares to cover the box. Leave it in a warm airy spot to dry.

3 When the paint is completely dry, the box is ready to decorate. Cut carefully around the pictures, glue on the border and then the feature picture.

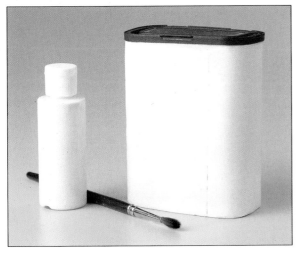

2 When the papier-mâché layer is dry, paint on a base coat of color. You may need two coats to make a good surface to decorate.

4 When the glue is set, the box is ready to varnish. It will need two coats to give it a professional finish.

Decorate small wooden boxes to use for jewelry. Clean up the wood with sandpaper first, then glue on your pictures. Apply two coats of varnish when the glue is dry.

Jewelry Box

Keep your jewelry safe in one of these sparkling treasure troves. The boxes are made from thick card and decorated with gold and silver paint, glitter, glass beads and recycled junk jewelry. If you don't have any suitable old jewels, use brightly decorated gold or silver buttons or sequins.

You will need:

Thick card

Scissors

Sticky tape and glue

Newspaper

Gold paint and glitter

Shiny buttons or jewelry to recycle

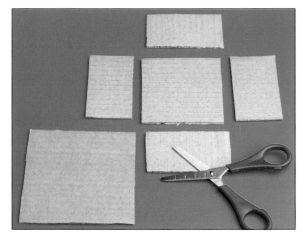

1 Cut a base and lid from thick card. Use the base to measure the size of the walls of the box.

3 Glue two layers of squares cut from the newspaper onto the box and lid. Leave in a warm airy spot to dry.

2 Stick the shapes together to form the box. Use glue or tape.

4 When the papier-mâché layer is dry, it is ready to decorate. Paint the box inside and out with gold paint. It may need two coats. When the paint is dry, decorate the lid with glitter, paint, and jewels.

Remember to protect the work surface with newspaper before you begin.

MATCHBOX
Chest of Drawers

The decorations on these tiny chests of drawers give you a good idea of the contents. The chests of drawers are useful for storing stamps or buttons and are made from empty matchboxes, covered with sticky-backed paper. You may want to make a set of drawers for the toolbox to store small nails and screws. The button drawers would be good for saving odd buttons from the sewing box and stamp collectors would find the stamp drawers very useful. You could even make a tiny chest of drawers and decorate it to put in the dollhouse bedroom.

You will need:

Empty matchboxes

Glue

Scissors

Sticky-backed paper

Felt

Selection of buttons and stamps

Thin wire (fuse wire would do well)

Saucer of water

Paper fasteners

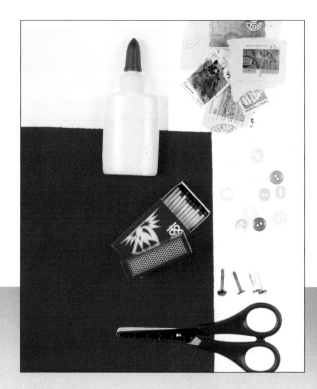

1 To make the button storage drawers, begin by gluing the three matchboxes, one on top of another. When the glue has dried, cover the set of drawers with sticky-backed paper. Spread the box with glue, then stick on the felt covering. Dab on a little glue and stick on the buttons, one at a time. To make handles for the drawers, attach buttons with a little wire.

2 To make the stamp drawer you will need a selection of brightly decorated stamps. Place the stamps in a saucer of water for a few minutes to loosen the glue and remove them from the envelope paper. Glue three matchboxes one on top of another then cover the box with sticky-backed paper. Glue on the stamps, taking care to arrange them so you can see the interesting pictures on them. Make drawer handles from paper fasteners.

You could use stickers to decorate a chest of drawers or decorate the sticky-backed paper with felt-tip pens.

Money Boxes

hese stylishly decorated money boxes would look good in the living room. They are made from recycled containers which have good, well-fitting lids. Encourage the whole family to make savings by decorating money boxes for them all. Flowers painted pink, bright orange and yellow, or a money box that suits a particular hobby or style—you can create them easily from old boxes.

You will need:

Sturdy containers with well-fitting lids

Scissors

Newspaper

Glue

Paint

Paintbrushes

1 You will need an adult to help you cut out the money slit. Use a large coin to help measure the space.

3 When the papier-mâché is dry, paint on the base colour, then paint on tiny trees and shrubs.

2 Glue squares of newspaper onto the box to make a good painting surface.

4 These money boxes are made from cardboard boxes. Cut out a slit before covering completely with papier-mâché. Once full they will need to be cut open to get at the money!

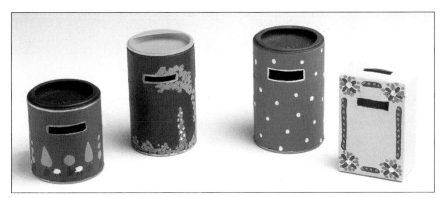

Origami

Paper folding is a useful skill to learn. Follow the instructions and once you have mastered them, if you have a sheet of paper, you will never be without a box. Use stiff cardboard to make a large box and small sheets of paper to make a smaller one. Origami boxes can be used to store party favors, candies, and odds and ends. A sturdy, cardboard-folded box could be used as a simple tray to hold cookies. Have a go, all you need is a sheet of paper and a little practice.

You will need:

Paper in a selection of colors and weights

1 Fold the paper in half lengthwise.

4 Fold in the corners and tuck them under the small fold.

2 Fold each half into the middle.

5 Place your fingers in the corners and lift the box into shape.

3 Make a small fold back outward on both sides.

When paper folding, be sure to press the folds firmly so they are sharp.

CARDBOARD
Pencil Cases

Make yourself a shimmering, space age pencil case with paper, paint, and glitter. Find a container tall enough to carry a ruler and make sure it has a well-fitting lid. An empty spaghetti container or potato chip box could be recycled to make a good pencil case. Once you have glued on a layer of papier mâché your pencil case is ready for decoration. You could create a theme pencil case to match a favourite pen or your book covers and schoolbag.

You will need:
Tall containers with tightly fitting lids

Newspaper

Glue

Scissors

Paint

Paintbrushes

Glitter

1 Clean the container and check that your pens, pencils, and ruler will fit in. Make sure the lid fits well.

Cover the box with a layer of newspaper squares, glued on. Leave in a warm, airy spot to dry.

2 When the papier-mâché layer is completely dry, the pencil case is ready to decorate. Paint it with a base coat then decorate it with space ships, shiny stars and glitter.

Remember to protect your work surface with newspaper before you begin.

When using glitter, place a sheet of paper under your model before sprinkling the glitter. Pour any excess glitter back into the container.

CARDBOARD TUBE
Pencil Tubs

Use paint and glitter to decorate a useful storage tub for pens and pencils. Choose a cylinder-shaped container to recycle into a pencil tub and cover it with a layer of papier-mâché to make it stronger and provide a good surface to decorate.

You will need:

Cardboard containers

Newspaper

Glue

Paint

Glitter

Paintbrushes

Scissors

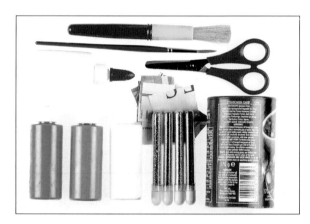

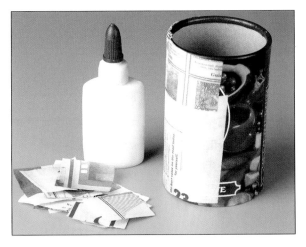

1 Start by covering the container with a layer of newspaper squares, glued on. Cover the container and leave it in a warm, airy place to dry.

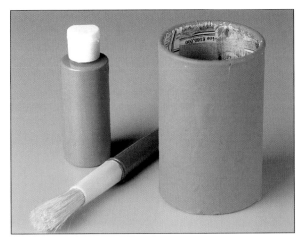

2 When the papier-mâché is completely dry, paint on a base coat and allow it to dry. You may need two coats of paint.

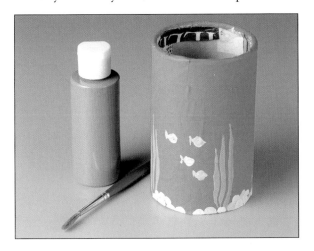

3 Paint on the fish and seaweed, using one color at a time. Don't forget to paint on some air bubbles above the fish.

4 When the paint is dry, spread glue on areas you want to glitter and sprinkle on the glitter. Do this one color at a time and leave it to dry between colors.

Before you begin, give the cardboard container a quick wash. Stand it upside down to drain and then dry it with a clean dishtowel.

Fabric-covered
Sewing Box

Keep needles and pins, thread and scissors safely to hand in this pretty, fabric-covered sewing box. The box is made from two layers of thick cardboard, each covered with polyester wadding and fabric, and then glued together. When you have mastered the technique you could make a small travel sewing box to match your home sewing box. A fabric-covered box could also be used to hold handkerchiefs, hairbands, and scrunchies.

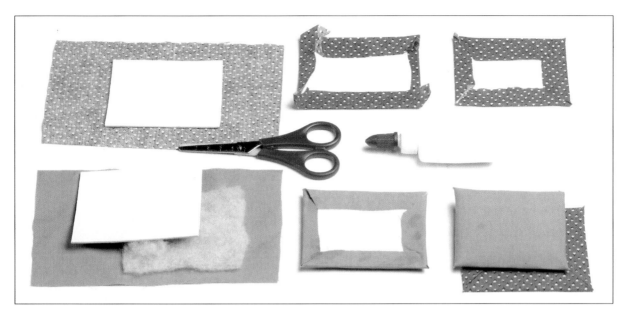

1 Cut the base from thick cardboard. Use this to measure out the sides of the box and cut the lid the same size as the base. This will be the outer box. Cut out two complete sets of cardboard. Now cut one quarter of an inch off around the edge of one set of cardboard pieces. This will be the inner box.

2 Glue a piece of wadding to the four sides of the outer box and cover each one with patterned fabric. Cover the outer lid and base pieces with patterned fabric. Glue a piece of wadding to each piece of the inner box, including the lid and base, then cover these with plain fabric. (Choose co-ordinating fabrics for a stylish effect.)

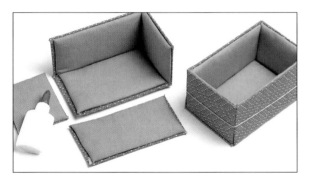

3 Glue the matching outer and inner pieces together. Glue the whole box together and hold it in place with the rubber band.

You will need:

Thick cardboard

Scissors

Wadding

20 inches of patterned fabric

Fabric glue

20 inches of plain fabric

A rubber band

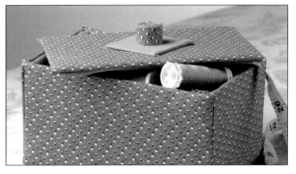

4 To decorate the lid, cover a small square piece of cardboard with plain fabric. Glue this on to the lid. Now cut a strip of fabric, cover it with glue and fold it in half lengthways, roll it up to form a grip, and glue it on to the lid.

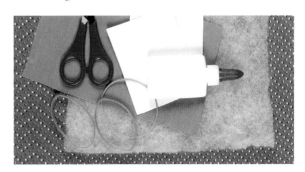

Tissue Box Covers

Brighten up a box of tissues with a cover decorated with spring flowers made from colored paper and cardboard. A daffodil-covered tissue box would make a cheery get-well gift for a friend or relative. Once you have mastered the technique you could decorate cardboard with a bunch of daffodils to go with the tissue box. A small posy of colored flowers would look good on a square tissue box.

You will need:

Thick colored cardboard

Scissors

Tape

Colored paper

Glue

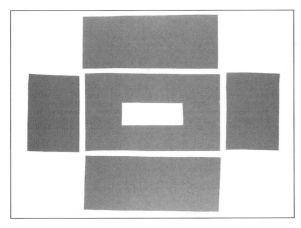

1 Use the tissue box as a pattern and cut out the four sides and top of the cover. Ask an adult to cut a wide slit for the tissues to pull through.

4 Shape the fringed strip into the center of the flower by winding it around your finger. Then glue it in place. Check that the pieces form a well-shaped flower.

2 Use tape to hold the box together. Cover the tape with decorative edging, cut from colored paper and stuck on with glue.

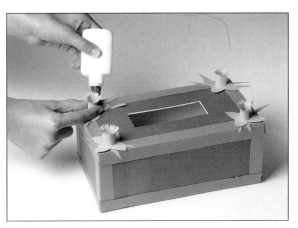

5 Glue the flowers and leaves to your finished tissue box cover. Well done!

3 Cut out the petal shape from yellow paper. Cut out some green leaves. Cut a fringed strip to make the center of the flower.

Cut out and make a few flowers and use the best ones to decorate your tissue box cover. Practice makes perfect!

CARDBOARD
Toy Boxes

Keep your toys and games tidy in one of these stylishly stenciled toy boxes. Use colors and designs that match your bedroom and make stencils easily from sheets of paper. A nicely stenciled toy box would make a good gift for a younger brother or sister, and older family members might like a well-decorated box to use as a storage container.

You will need rather a lot of glue and paint to cover a grocery box. Check with an adult before you begin to make sure you have enough.

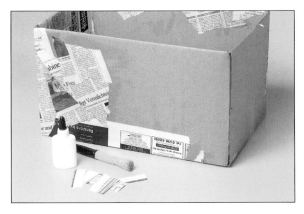

1 Cover the grocery box, inside and out, with two layers of newspaper, glued on. Do this in stages, allowing the box to dry in a warm, airy place between layers.

3 Draw your stencil design onto the center of a sheet of paper and cut it out carefully. You may want to make a few stencils and try them out on scrap paper.

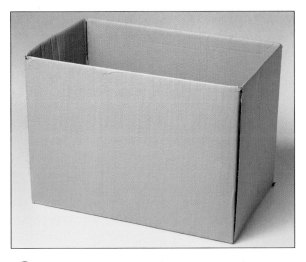

2 When the papier mâché layer is dry, paint the box. Sometimes a second coat of paint is needed to cover the newspaper. Let the paint dry between coats.

4 Hold the stencil on the box. Dip the sponge into a little paint and pat it on the saucer. Practice on scrap paper before decorating your toy box.

You will need:

Grocery box

Glue

Newspaper

Paint

Paintbrushes

Paper

Scissors

Sponge

Saucer

Wastebaskets

Let these brightly colored wastebaskets inspire you to make a tidy version for every room in the house. The wastebaskets are made from cardboard and easily decorated with wrapping paper for a very stylish finish. Big sister will like the gold-colored basket and the floral one will look good in the bathroom. The dotty wastebasket will brighten the hall and I'm sure you know someone who would love a dinosaur-covered one.

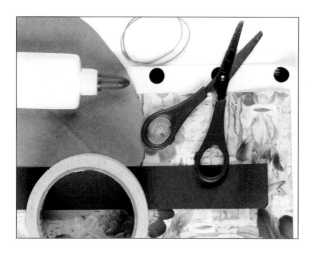

You will need:

Pencil

Thick cardboard

Scissors

Stiff cardboard

Rubber band

Glue

Masking tape

Wrapping paper

Colored paper

1 Begin by making the base of the box. Draw an oval shape onto thick cardboard (recycled cardboard from a grocery box would be good) and cut it out.

3 Put some glue around the edge of the base. Cut a piece of masking tape the height of the rim and attach it to one side of the wall of the basket.

2 Cut out the wall of the basket from stiff cardboard. Use the base to measure how long it should be. Shape it into a cylinder and hold it in place with the rubber band.

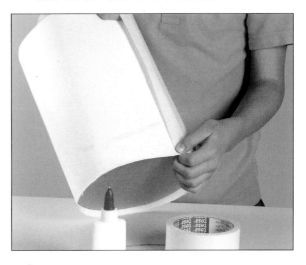

4 Wind the wall around the base and hold it in place with the masking tape.

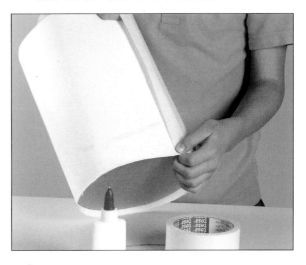

5 Your basket is now ready to decorate with wrapping paper or dinosaur cutouts.

Woodland Cottage

This little log cottage is just waiting for someone to visit and enjoy the pastries and apples set out on the table. The cottage is made from a grocery box and corrugated cardboard. The flowers on the front of the cottage are made from scrunched-up scraps of tissue paper, glued directly on to the walls. When you have made the model, you might try your hand at making some furnishings to put inside the woodland cottage.

You will need:

Corrugated and thick card

Tape

Scissors

Glue

Newspaper

Paint and paintbrushes

Colored tissue paper

Some plastic potted plants

Oven-bake clay

Small rolling pin

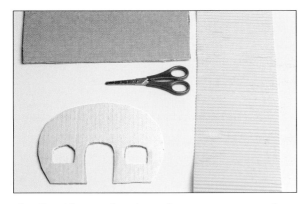

1 Decide on the size of your cottage and cut out the base from thick cardboard. Next cut out a front for the cottage. Ask an adult to help if you have difficulty. Cut out the windows and door. Use a wide strip of corrugated cardboard to shape the rest of the cottage.

2 Tape the cottage into shape. You may need a little help, one pair of hands to hold things and another pair to attach the tape.

3 Cover the entire model with two layers of newspaper squares, glued on. Leave it in a warm airy place until it is dry.

4 Paint the house, allowing each color to dry before you start on the next one. Use crumpled-up pieces of tissue paper to decorate the house, choosing different colors for the various flowers, and green for leaves. A few plastic plants will give your woodland cottage a realistic feel.

5 The furnishings are made from oven-bake clay. Roll it out on a clean surface and shape the log-style bench and table. Make some tiny pastries to put on the table.

If you don't have any oven-bake clay, use Plasticine to make the furnishings and food.

CARDBOARD
Trinket Boxes

Boxes are great fun to make. These are painted and decorated with glass beads, paints, and glitter. Make a box to store your earrings, rings, and other small treasures. The square and rectangular boxes are made from recycled grocery box cardboard and the heart-shaped and oval boxes are made from corrugated cardboard. You can sometimes find this as packing or it can be bought in bright colors from a craft shop. The decoration on your box could give a clue as to what is inside it!

You will need:
Thick cardboard
Scissors
Tape
Newspaper
Glue
Paint
Paintbrushes
Corrugated cardboard
Tissue paper
Glitter or glass beads

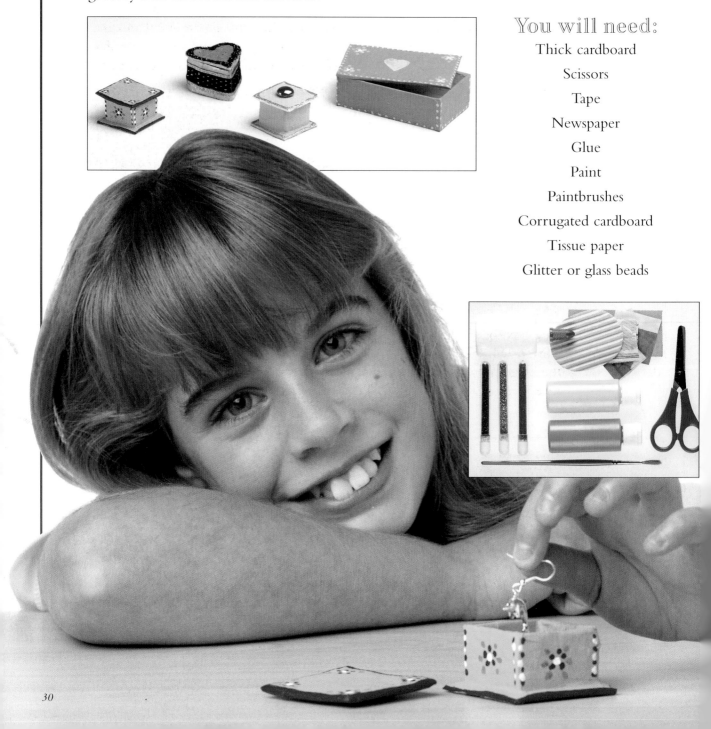

1 Use cardboard from a grocery box. Decide on the size of your box, then measure out a base and sides. The lid is made from two squares of cardboard, one smaller than the other.

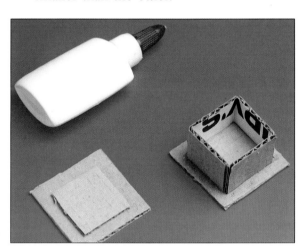

2 Use tape to hold the box together and make sure the lid fits. It will need to be the same size as the base, and the smaller piece of cardboard will need to fit into the box.

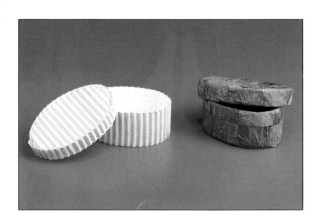

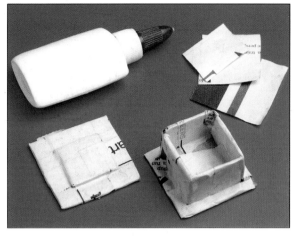

3 Cover the box with a layer of papier-mâché made from newspaper squares, glued on. Check the lid fits and then leave the box and lid in a warm airy spot to dry before you begin to decorate it with paint.

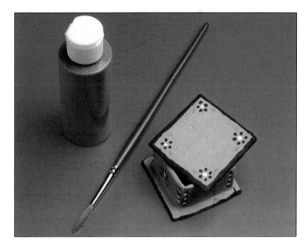

4 When the papier-mâché is dry, paint a base coat of color. You may need to give the box a second coat of paint. Use the point of the brush to paint flowers and leaves on the box and lid, and paint a bright red border.

5 This oval box is made from corrugated cardboard which is easy to bend. Cut an oval shape for the base. The lid will need to be larger than the base, so it fits over the side. This box is covered with colored tissue paper. Decorate the edge of a heart-shaped box with glitter or glass beads.

Index